# UNCOVERING THE PAST

# THE DISPLACEMENT OF NATIVE PEOPLES

## LYNN LESLIE PEPPAS

 Crabtree Publishing Company

www.crabtreebooks.com

**Author:** Lynn Leslie Peppas
**Publishing plan research and development:**
   Reagan Miller
**Editor-in-chief:** Lionel Bender
**Editors:** Simon Adams, Anastasia Suen
**Content review:** Janine Deschenes
**Proofreaders:** Laura Booth, Petrice Custance
**Project coordinator:** Kathy Middleton
**Design and photo research:** Ben White
**Cover design:** Ken Wright
**Production coordinator and prepress
   technician:** Samara Parent
**Print coordinator:** Margaret Amy Salter
**Production coordinated by:** Bender
   Richardson White

**Consultants:**
Amie Wright, The New York Public Library;
Diane Glancy, M.A. Eng. M.A. Fine Arts.
Poet, author, playwright, English professor,
and teacher of Native American literature
and creative writing;
Dr. Pamela Rose Toulouse, Associate
Professor, School of Education at Laurentian
University, author of Achieving Aboriginal
Student Success: A Guide for K to 8
Classrooms

**Photographs and reproductions:**
Photographs: Corbis: 41 (Miguel Juarez Lugo/ZUMA Press), 36 (Robert Giroux),
37 (Maggie Steber), 38–39 (AFP PHOTO/BULENT KILIC), 40 (KIM
STALLKNECHT AFP); Library of Congress: cover, 1 (LC-USZC4-510), 3 (LC-
USZ62-77909), 4, 6 Icon (LC-USZC4-3163), 6 (LC-USZC4-1490), 8, 10, 12 Icon
(LC-USZC4-510), 14, 16 Icon (LC-USZ62-107815), 17 (LC-DIG-pga-07569), 18, 20,
22, 24, 26, 28, 30, 32 Icon (LC-USZ62-77909), 23 (mjm.12_0579_0586), 25
(g4021e.ct000224), 26–27 (LC-DIG-pga-07513), 34, 36 Icon (LC-USZ62-26785);
Shutterstock: 38, 40 Icon (Paul McKinnon); Topfoto: 4–5 (The Granger Collection),
7 (World History Archive), 8–9 (The Granger Collection), 10 (The Granger
Collection), 11 (The Granger Collection), 12 (D. LADA/ClassicStock), 13 (World
History Archive), 14–15 (The Granger Collection), 16 (The Granger Collection),
16–17 (United Archives), 18–19 (The Granger Collection), 20 (World History
Archive), 22 (World History Archive), 24 (The Granger Collection), 27 (The
Granger Collection), 28 (The Granger Collection), 29 (Roger-Viollet), 30 (The
Granger Collection), 31 (The Granger Collection), 32 (The Granger Collection),
33 (The Granger Collection), 34–35 (The Granger Collection),
35 (Artmedia/Heritage Images).
Graphics: Stephan Chabluk

**Cover photo:** Painting by John Gast in 1872 represents the westward expansion of
the United States.
**Title page photo:** Painting by J.O. Lewis shows Natives from many tribes and
U.S. military encampment at Prairie du Chien for the presentation of the treaty in
September 1825.

**Library and Archives Canada Cataloguing in Publication**

Peppas, Lynn, author
      The displacement of native peoples / Lynn Peppas.

(Uncovering the past: analyzing primary sources)
Includes bibliographical references and index.
Issued in print and electronic formats.
ISBN 978-0-7787-2571-8 (bound).--ISBN 978-0-7787-2573-2 (paperback).--
ISBN 978-1-4271-1761-8 (html)

      1. Indians, Treatment of--Canada--History--Sources--Juvenile
literature.  2. Indians, Treatment of--United States--History--Sources--
Juvenile literature.  3. Indians of North America--Canada--Government
relations--History--Sources--Juvenile literature.  4. Indians of North
America--United States--Government relations--History--Sources--
Juvenile literature.  I. Title.

E91.P47 2016           j970.004'97           C2015-907984-5
                                             C2015-907985-3

**Library of Congress Cataloguing in Publication**

CIP available at Library of Congress

# Crabtree Publishing Company

Printed in Canada/022016/MA20151130

www.crabtreebooks.com          1-800-387-7650

**Published in Canada**
**Crabtree Publishing**
616 Welland Ave.
St. Catharines, Ontario
L2M 5V6

**Published in the**
**United States**
**Crabtree Publishing**
PMB 59051
350 Fifth Avenue, 59th Floor
New York, NY 10118

**Published in the**
**United Kingdom**
**Crabtree Publishing**
Maritine House
Basin Road North, Hove
BN4 1WR

**Published in Australia**
**Crabtree Publishing**
3 Charles Street
Coburg North
VIC 3058

# UNCOVERING THE PAST

# THE PAST COMES ALIVE

*"Our property may be plundered before our eyes; violence may be committed on our persons; even our lives may be taken away, and there is none to regard our complaints. . . . We have neither land nor home, nor resting place that can be called our own."*

Cherokee chief John Ross, September 18, 1836

Historians estimate that about 10 million Native peoples lived in North America for about 30,000 years before European **immigrants** began to colonize the continent in the 1600s. Contact with the Europeans drastically changed the Native peoples' ways of life. Millions died from European diseases. Those who did survive later lost their homelands and their culture.

But have you ever wondered how historians know all about this? Unless a person has lived through a period of time, or actually witnessed an event, they cannot know what truly happened in the past. **History,** however, is different from the past. History is a collection of recorded and preserved **documents**, records, and **artifacts** called **primary sources.**

**Historians** work in much the same way as detectives do. They gather and study primary sources to find clues or pieces of **evidence** and put together the story of what really happened.

It is important to study the past so we don't make the same mistakes twice. People are people—whether they lived 500 years ago or today—and we often deal with very similar problems. By studying what has and has not worked in the past, we can put together a plan of action to solve a problem or prevent one from ever occurring again!

▶ Powhatan chief Opechancanough organized and led a union of Native peoples in two rebellions against the English colonists of Virginia in 1622 and 1644. He was killed while being held captive by English colonists in 1646.

## EVIDENCE RECORD CARD

Opechancanough in a
meeting with the colonial
governor of Virginia
**LEVEL** Secondary source
**MATERIAL** Hand-colored
engraving
**LOCATION** Virginia
**DATE** 1877
**SOURCE** Topfoto

## ANALYZE THIS

This image of Opechancanough in a meeting with the colonial English governor and an official of Virginia was created in 1877, over 230 years after Opechancanough's death. European peoples created the myth that Native peoples were savages and not **civilized**. How has the artist chosen to portray Opechancanough differently from the colonists? What does the artist want you to think about Opechancanough? Do you think this image was created to make the viewer believe Native peoples were savages?

## PERSPECTIVES

Often we absorb other peoples' opinions from TV shows, books, and magazines, or on websites. But remember, not everything you read or see is true. Only primary sources give you evidence of the past. So, try to forget what you think you know about Native peoples in North America and investigate primary sources to come up with your own understanding of what really happened. Your investigative work may reveal something new about the past that has not yet been discovered!

## EUROPEAN CONTACT

Before the Europeans settled in North America, thousands of tribes of Native peoples lived within their own systems of religion and government. Native peoples had weapons and tools. Their communities were organized. They built homes and raised families. Some tribes farmed and others fought wars. They had beliefs about how people should behave with each other. Native peoples were in every way civilized.

European explorers arrived in North America more than 500 years ago. They called it the New World and claimed the land as **colonies** of their **homelands**, namely Spain, Great Britain, and France. The opportunity to **export** the New World's **resources** back to Europe and **convert** the New World's Native peoples to **Christianity** brought more European **colonists**.

First contact between Europeans and Native peoples introduced a number of European diseases, such as smallpox and measles, to large populations of Native peoples who had no **immunity** to them. Historians estimate that millions of Native peoples died. In some cases, entire nations of Native peoples were wiped out.

After European contact, Native peoples were systematically **displaced** from their homelands by governments in favor of European settlers. Throughout the 1800s

### ANALYZE THIS

There is no mention of Native peoples in this illustrated chart, but they can be seen hiding from landed **pilgrims** to the left side of this tree. It is dedicated to the "People of the United States." Do you think that this artist, drawing this image in 1881, thought of Native peoples as peoples of the United States? Why or why not?

CHRONOLOGICAL CHART OF AMERICAN HISTORY.
DEDICATED TO THE
PEOPLE OF THE UNITED STATES
BY THE PUBLISHER.

*"What is this you call property? It cannot be earth, for the land is our mother, nourishing all her children, beasts, birds, fish, and all men. The woods, the streams, everything on it belongs to everybody and is for the use of all. How can one man say it belongs only to him?"*

Massasoit, leader of the Wampanoag, circa 1600

▲ This historical chart was first published in 1881 and shows a record of American events that begins with the arrival in the Americas of Christopher Columbus in 1492.

to 1900s, both Canadian and American governments worked toward **assimilating** Native peoples so that they would become more "civilized." By "civilized," each government meant that all Native peoples should act like and share the same **culture** as the European colonists. Some Native peoples tried to become like the colonists, while others fought against them. Native peoples' struggles with their loss of land and culture continue to this day.

▼ British artist, John White, painted the *Indian Ritual Dance* around 1585. White was the governor of an early colony in the New World, but the colony failed. He was hired to paint life scenes of the Native peoples living in the New World.

## DEFINITIONS

Throughout history, Native peoples in North America have been referred to by different names. Some terms are offensive and should never be used. However, these terms were used hundreds of years ago in primary sources, and for this reason have been included for **context** only.

**Aboriginal:** A race of people and their descendants who have lived in an area from earliest times.

**American Indian or Indian:** Christopher Columbus thought he had landed in India and wrongly referred to the Native peoples of North America as "Indians;" in Canada, the name is considered offensive.

**First Nations:** Native peoples of Canada who are not Métis (people of mixed Aboriginal and European descent) or Inuit (aboriginal Canadians living in the far north); the term is frequently used in Canada and less so in the United States.

**First Peoples:** Aboriginal peoples living in North America.

**Indigenous:** Originating from, and belonging to, an area or place.

**Inuit:** Indigenous peoples of Northern Canada who speak Inuktitut.

**Métis:** A person of mixed indigenous and European ancestry.

**Native:** (adj) Born in a particular area or place; (noun) to refer to a person as a "native" is considered outdated.

**Native American:** This term originated in the 1960s to replace the term American Indian, in the same way that African American was coined.

**Redskin:** An offensive term for Native peoples that has been used for hundreds of years, outdated today with the exception of American sports teams.

**Savage:** (adj) Wild and untamed; (noun) an offensive term used in the 1700s and 1800s by Europeans to label Native peoples, especially those who were not Christian.

**Squaw:** An offensive name for a young, aboriginal female.

HISTORICAL SOURCES

# EVIDENCE FROM THE PAST

*". . . as we waded through the shallow water, we saw a wild and striking scene. . . . On the farther bank stood a large and strong man, nearly naked, holding a white horse by a long cord, and eyeing us as we approached. This was the chief, whom Henry called 'Old Smoke.' Just behind him his youngest and favorite squaw sat astride of a fine mule."*

Excerpt from *The Oregon Trail* by Francis Parkman, published circa 1846

A primary source is a piece of evidence that has been kept, or preserved, and handed down from the past. To find out if it is a primary source or not, ask yourself this question: Did a person who witnessed an **era** or event create it? If the answer is yes, then it is a primary source. Primary sources come in different forms such as a written document, artifact, or a person's recorded memory of an event. They give the best clues as to what really occurred in the past. Primary sources supply the most reliable source of historical information.

You create primary sources every day, such as journal entries, homework assignments, emails or texts to friends, Facebook posts, or photos you take. These examples may serve as evidence for a historian hundreds of years from now. Imagine what could be figured out about what people your age were like just by looking at the primary sources you've created!

▶ **The Greenville Treaty (1795) shows the X marks or signatures of some of the Native leaders who signed it. The treaty brought peace between European and some Native nations. However, these nations had to give up their claims to tribal lands in the Northwest Territory, which is now part of Canada.**

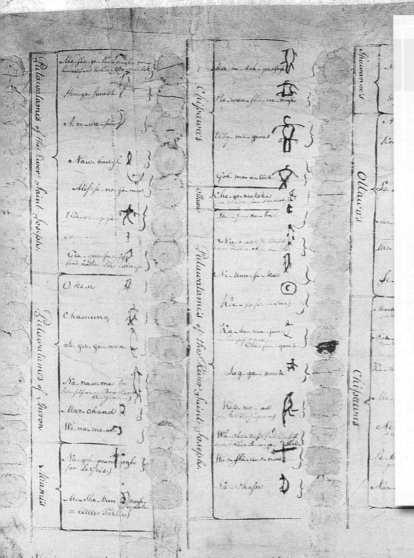

## EVIDENCE RECORD CARD

Greenville Treaty
**LEVEL** Primary source
**MATERIAL** Paper document
**LOCATION** Ohio
**DATE** 1795
**SOURCE** Topfoto

## SECONDARY SOURCES

A **secondary source** is one person's description or interpretation of a historical event or era. A person who produces a secondary source did not participate in or witness the event or era. Authors, artists, and historians create secondary sources by investigating, interpreting, and evaluating primary sources from the past.

For example, a historical novel such as American writer James Fenimore Cooper's *The Last of the Mohicans: A Narrative of 1757* was published in 1826. The novel is set in 1757 but Cooper was, in fact, born years later, in 1789. To determine if a source is primary or secondary, always ask yourself: Was the person creating the source present or not? Cooper obviously was not present during 1757, so this makes *The Last of the Mohicans* a secondary source.

### ANALYZE THIS

American political cartoonist Thomas Nast published *Every Dog (No Distinction of Color) Has His Day* in 1879. How has Nast represented each figure's cultural background in this cartoon? Do you think Nast sympathizes with his characters? What did the Chinese-Americans, Native peoples, and African-Americans have in common in the 1870s?

◀ This cartoon of 1879 by Thomas Nast, called *Every Dog (No Distinction of Color) Has His Day*, shows people from three racial minorities examining the conflicting racial messages of the day.

"A long time ago this land belonged to our fathers; but when I go up to the river I see camps of soldiers here on its bank. These soldiers cut down my timber; they kill my buffalo; and when I see that, my heart feels like bursting; I feel sorry."

Santana, chief of the Kiowas, 1867, from the *U.S. Bureau of Ethnography Annual Report*, 17th edition, 1895–1896

## WHAT IS A SECONDARY SOURCE?

Secondary sources have used one or more primary sources to form opinions or reach conclusions. They have collected evidence and interpreted it for you already. Secondary sources include:
- Encyclopedias
- Textbooks
- Newspaper or magazine articles about an event in the past
- Maps created today to show historical information
- Internet websites
- Interview of an expert on a topic who did not directly experience the situation or event

▼ This oil painting is by the artist Robert Lindneux. It is titled *The Trail of Tears* and shows the removal of the Cherokee Native Americans to the West in 1838.

## FINDING RELIABLE SOURCES

Primary sources are always more **reliable** sources of historical information than secondary sources. But some primary sources are considered to be better than others. This also holds true for secondary sources. The best primary or secondary sources are those created closest in time to the historical event under consideration.

For example, if a witness gave an account minutes after an event happened, it would be fresh in their memory and considered a very reliable primary source. But if that same person was interviewed 30 years later, their

### PERSPECTIVES

This photograph of Native peoples was most likely taken in the late 1900s or early 2000s. It is therefore a secondary source when searching for information about traditional clothing for Native peoples.

▲ Native peoples celebrate their culture with pow wows, or social gatherings. Today's pow wows feature dance competitions, music, storytelling, traditional foods, and cultural demonstrations.

account would still be considered a primary source, but the earlier account would be the more reliable of the two.

A secondary source created closest to the time a historical event occurred is a more reliable source of information than one created later. For example, Cooper's historical novel, *The Last of the Mohicans*, is a better secondary source than the novel *Dances with Wolves*, written by the American writer Michael Blake and published in 1988. Although both authors most likely studied primary sources to produce historical fictions with Aboriginal characters, Cooper lived closer to the era he was writing about than Blake did, so Cooper's novel is a more reliable source than Blake's.

◄ Two Sioux men, believed to be William Holy Frog (left) and Luke Big Turnips (right), were photographed around 1900 by American photographer Gertrude Kasebier. Both men may have been a part of Buffalo Bill's famous Wild West Show.

*"So far as can be judged the original Indian . . . was not naturally inclined to hostility toward the new-comers, and was, in fact, more disposed to hospitality."*

Excerpt from *The Story of the Dominion* by John Castell Hopkins, published in 1901

# AUDIENCE AND PURPOSE

*"They told us that Indian ways were bad. They said we must get civilized. I remember that word too. It means 'be like the white man.' . . . And the books told how bad the Indians had been to the white men—burning their towns and killing their women and children. But I had seen white men do that to Indians. . . . And so, after a while we also began to say Indians were bad."*

Sun Elk, educated at a reservation school in
Carlisle, Pennsylvania, in 1883

All primary sources are created for specific reasons. After you determine that you are looking at a primary source, ask yourself questions about it. This helps you understand the source better. It provides context—the time and place—of a primary source and helps you figure out what it means historically.

- What is the source, and who created it?
- Why was this source created?
- When, and where, was this source created?
- What does the source prove, claim, show, or say?
- What else was going on around the same time?

Consider the quotation given above. Sun Elk says that he saw "white" men do the very thing that Native peoples were accused of doing to white people, which was to "kill" and "burn." Here is an eyewitness account that violence was used on Native peoples, too. And the final sentences prove that the **reservation** school did change Sun Elk to be more "like the white man" and agree that "Indians were bad." Accounts such as these are clues as to how truthful the teachers and textbooks were during the late 1800s at reservation schools, and how these schools assimilated Native peoples and changed their beliefs.

▲ This oil painting, by John Jarvis, of the American Sauk Indian leader Black Hawk (1767–1838), right, with his son, left, was painted in 1833.

## PERSPECTIVES

John Jarvis painted this portrait while Black Hawk and his son were being
held prisoner by the U.S. government. A Wisconsin newspaper, *The
Commonwealth,* dated July 2, 1833, reported that: "Black Hawk attracts
almost as great a crowd as the President . . . (Black Hawk) walks out
upon balconies, and bows to the multitude with (exceptional) grace."
Considering the quote and the painting, what kind of personality do you
think Black Hawk might have had?

## CONSIDERING BIAS

All sources, primary or secondary, have some form of **bias.** Bias is the outlook or opinions a person has. Bias is not a bad thing, but it must be considered when analyzing a source.

For example, let us look for bias in the quotation below from Francis Parkman's *The Oregon Trail.* Francis Parkman was a wealthy, male, American history writer, who lived in Boston, Mass. He graduated from Harvard College in the mid–1800s and wrote about his travels throughout the United States. Parkman described the cultural fashion and dress of various Native nations when he visited Westport, Missouri, in 1846.

### ANALYZE THIS

This illustration was drawn and published for a later edition of *The Last of the Mohicans*, 46 years after its first publication. What do both men appear to be doing in the illustration? How are they different? How are they similar? What might both of these men be doing? Do you think they are working together?

THE
# LAST OF THE MOHICANS.

BY
JAMES FENIMORE COOPER.

NEW YORK:
D. APPLETON AND COMPANY, PUBLISHERS.

▲ This illustration in *The Last of the Mohicans* was drawn by Felix Octavius Carr Darley and published in a later 1872 edition.

"*Westport was full of Indians, whose little shaggy ponies were tied by dozens along the houses and fences. Sacs and Foxes, with shaved heads and painted faces, Shawanoes and Delawares, fluttering in calico frocks, and turbans, Wyandottes dressed like white men, and a few wretched Kansas wrapped in old blankets, were strolling about the streets, or lounging in and out of the shops and houses.*"

From *The Oregon Trail* by Francis Parkman, 1846

He identified different nations by their clothing. Were his statements correct? We must ask ourselves if the Kansas were truly "**wretched**," or simply appeared so because of their fashion choice. Were the Wyandottes, who were "dressed like white men," less wretched? Parkman has brought his upbringing, education, and personal opinions into the writing of his book. Uncovering a source's bias helps us to better understand and analyze the source's account of events.

Language is another point to consider when analyzing sources. People of European ancestry recorded most primary and secondary sources—government **treaties**, personal accounts, and documents—in English. But many Native peoples did not read or write in English, and there were many different Native languages and means of communication. These included the use of **wampum beads** to symbolize agreements. **Interpreters** often communicated ideas between two parties who spoke different languages. Native nations often signed treaties that they could not fully understand.

▲ The movie *The Last of the Mohicans* was released in 1992. The film was rated number one at the box office during its opening weekend and brought in more than $10 million.

◄ Sequoyah was the creator of the first Cherokee alphabet.

## PERSPECTIVES

A Cherokee named Sequoyah created the Cherokee alphabet in the early 1800s so that his nation could read, write, and record written documents. Can you read the letters written on this page? Why or why not?

# DISPLACEMENT

*"P.S. I will try to inoculate the Indians by means of blankets that may fall in their hands, taking care however not to get the disease myself."*

In a letter written to General Amherst, July 13, 1763, Colonel Henry Bouquet describes a method of exterminating Native populations by spreading smallpox

Europeans who arrived in North America in the 1600s called it the New World. But for the Native peoples who had lived there for tens of thousands of years, it was their homeland.

Native peoples believed that land could never be owned by one person or a group of people, and could o[...] shared. Most Native nations held a spiritual or religious connection with Earth and nature[...]ey respected wildlife and never wasted any part of the animals they hunted for food. European hunters often killed for sport or slaughter, especially bison, or buffalo, and left the carcasses to rot.

The first major wave of **displacement** of Native peoples was linked to the American Revolution (1775–1783). This was a war for **independence** fought between rebellious European colonists (Patriots) and those Europeans loyal to Great Britain (Loyalists). Some Native nations remained **neutral.** Others fought for the Patriot or Loyalist sides. The Patriots won their independence from Great Britain in 1783. Since the new country had little money to pay Patriot soldiers, many were given grants of land in payment. The Native peop[...]ho were already living on this land were forced to leave. Land was also taken as a punishment by the new U.S. government from Native nations who had fought for the British Loyalists. About 30,000 Loyalists fled the United States for Canada. These Loyalists needed land, so land-surrender treaties were made by the British with Anishinaabeg (Ojibway) peoples living around the Great Lakes region.

▶ This scene of a Florida Native nations ceremony was sketched by Jacques le Moyne during an expedition to the New World around the 1560s. About 30 years later Theodor de Bry made an engraving of the image.

## PERSPECTIVES

Even though the Native nations lived civilized lives with their own governments and religious ceremonies, their civilizations did not look like the European model of civilization. Because of this, most Europeans believed that Native peoples were more like savages.

## WESTERN EXPANSION

After winning the American Revolution, Europeans believed they should own and occupy the entire continent of North America, from the Atlantic to the Pacific oceans. This idea was known as **Manifest Destiny**. The U.S. government turned its attention to expanding the country from the original 13 colonies by moving westward across the continent.

In the early 1800s, more than 100,000 Native peoples from different nations

---

### EVIDENCE RECORD CARD

*American Progress*
**LEVEL**  Primary source
**MATERIAL**  Print of a painting by John Gast
**LOCATION**  United States
**DATE**  1872
**SOURCE**  Library of Congress

---

▼ The floating woman shown in the center of the painting is "Columbia." She represents the progress of the United States.

---

### ANALYZE THIS

What color is the sky behind and before Columbia? What do you think this symbolizes? Do the European peoples appear to be settled and happy? What are the Native peoples doing and how do they feel?

---

lived on the East Coast of the United States. This was prime land for European immigrants. The U.S. government began signing treaties with Native nations that forced them from their homelands and relocated them to the West.

## WAR AND PEACE
Some Native peoples fought against relocation and refused to sign treaties that gave up their rights to live and hunt on their homelands. Other Native nations peacefully gave up their homelands and signed government treaties. In the end, Native peoples in the United States and Canada were forced to **relocate** to smaller areas of land to make room for European settlements, whether they did it peacefully or with varying degrees of resistance.

## PERSPECTIVES ON IMPACT OF CONTACT BETWEEN PEOPLES

**Positive impact of contact between Native peoples and Europeans in the 1600s**

**Pros for Native peoples**
Introduced to more advanced technologies such as weapons and metal tools, as well as the use of the horse for transportation and labor
Farm animals are introduced such as pigs, sheep, goats, and chickens

**Pros for Europeans**
Native peoples teach European settlers how to survive in the New World
New World provides land for new colonies
New sources of natural resources such as furs, metals, and lumber
Enslaved Native peoples provide source of labor
New World food crops introduced in Europe such as sweet potatoes, corn, potatoes, tomatoes, peppers, and tobacco
Opportunities for missionaries to convert Native peoples to Christianity

**Negative impact of contact between Native peoples and Europeans in the 1600s**

**Cons for Native peoples**
Europeans spread diseases such as smallpox, measles, whooping cough, chicken pox, bubonic plague, typhus, and malaria to Native nations who have no immunity to them; it is estimated that more than 50 percent of the population of Native peoples died of these diseases within the first 100 years of European contact
Millions die in conflicts, wars, and violent acts by European settlers
Native peoples are forced to move from their homelands and relocated to areas in which they do not want to live
European settlers create laws that force Native peoples to assimilate and lose their culture and traditions
Some European settlers enslave Native peoples
European peoples change the environment by farming, and allowing livestock to graze large areas; wildlife that Native peoples had depended on for food sources are endangered, some to the point of near-extinction
European settlers introduce alcohol to Native peoples

**Cons for Europeans**
Deaths due to conflicts, wars, and violent acts by Native peoples

## ANALYZE THIS

In your opinion, which culture benefited from contact and which culture suffered? Do you think this was fair? What are your ideas about how things could have been handled differently?

## ANALYZE THIS

Colonel Johnson is shown on a white horse in the center of the painting. Which figure do you think Tecumseh is? Do you think Native warriors actually wore matching uniforms like this? Given the year this painting was created, does this make the painting a primary or secondary source?

### BATTLE OF FALLEN TIMBERS

A **confederation** of Ohio Valley Native nations formed around 1790 in the Ohio area to protect Native peoples' lands from European settlement. War broke out between the U.S. government—which wanted to gain lands in the Ohio valley—and the Native Confederation led by Myaamia leader, Little Turtle, and Shawanwa (Shawnee) leader, Blue Jacket. The Ohio Valley Native Confederation defeated U.S. forces in two battles in 1790 and 1791. U.S. president George Washington then appointed a new general, Anthony Wayne, who led about 3,000 soldiers to fight the Ohio Valley Native Confederation. In August 1794 the U.S. forces defeated

*"Let the white race perish. They seize your land; they corrupt your women; they trample ashes of your dead! Back, whence they came, upon a trail of blood, they must be driven. . . . The Red Man owns the country, and the Palefaces must never enjoy it."*

Shawanwa (Shawnee) leader, Tecumseh, 1811

▲ *Battle of the Thames and the Death of Tecumseh* was painted by William Emmons in 1892.

the Native Confederacy in the Battle of Fallen Timbers. After the battle its troops destroyed surrounding Native peoples' villages as punishment. Little Turtle and Blue Jacket signed the Treaty of Greenville in 1795 that gave Ohio and parts of Indiana to the United States.

## TREATY OF FORT WAYNE

In 1809, the Treaty of Fort Wayne was signed between Indiana Territory governor William Henry Harrison and a number of Native nations' leaders from the Delaware, Shawanwa, Putawatimies, Kickapoo, and Miami nations. The treaty sold about 3 million acres of land to the U.S. government. But according to Native peoples beliefs, no one person or group owned specific areas of land. In 1810, the Shawanwa leader Tecumseh met with Harrison to argue that the Native peoples who signed the treaty had no right to sell the land. Harrison refused to budge.

Tecumseh formed a confederacy of Native warriors to fight against American expansion. Joining forces with the British to fight against the U.S. Army in the War of 1812, Techumseh was killed at the Battle of the Thames. Shortly after, his confederacy dissolved. Even though Native peoples fought alongside the British in battles during the war, they were not rewarded with territory in the Treaty of Ghent between the United States and Canada. Other nations fought against American soldiers in other wars, but none regained their lands.

**EVIDENCE RECORD CARD**

Transcription of a speech made by Tecumseh to Governor Harrison on August 20, 1810

**LEVEL** Primary source
**MATERIAL** Document
**LOCATION** Indiana Territory
**DATE** August 20, 1810
**SOURCE** Library of Congress

▶ Transcript of a speech by Tecumseh to Indiana Territory governor William Henry Harrison in 1810 to persuade him to undo the Treaty of Fort Wayne on the grounds that the Native leaders who signed it had no authority to do so.

## INDIAN REMOVAL ACT OF 1830

U.S. president Andrew Jackson signed the Indian Removal Act into law in 1830. The act gave the United States government the power to make removal treaties with Native nations living on land east of the Mississippi River that had not been settled by Europeans. The U.S. government could legally force Native peoples to move from their homelands to the Indian Territory west of the Mississippi River. Native peoples who wanted to stay had to be "civilized." This meant they had to act as the Europeans did, own and operate farms with African-American **slaves**, and live within their state laws. Native nations who peacefully signed treaties for removal were promised financial and material aid while traveling to their new homelands. Most never received the help they were promised in treaties, and many thousands died on the journey known as the Trail of Tears (see painting p 11).

### ANALYZE THIS

The original title of the print shown below is "Indians emigrating." Emigrating means to move from one country or region to another. Do you think that title represents what was happening at the time? Why or why not? Who was this image created for? How did these Cherokee peoples travel? What is the one Cherokee male in the far right corner carrying? How do the people in this print feel and do they seem content? Do you think this is a true depiction of the Cherokee displacement? Why or why not?

▶ This print of the Cherokee removal of 1838 was made from a wood engraving and used in an American textbook around 1850.

## ACCEPTANCE OR RESISTANCE TO DISPLACEMENT

Some Native peoples peacefully accepted displacement, such as the Chahta (Choctaws) peoples who signed the Treaty of Dancing Rabbit Creek in 1830. Of the thousands of Chahta peoples who left for the Indian Territory, hundreds died of starvation and exposure.

Many nations peacefully **negotiated** treaties to relocate, such as the Odawa (Ottawas), Wendat (Wyandots), Gayogohono (Cayugas), Onyota'aka (Oneidas), and others. U.S. soldiers forcefully removed individual nations and those Native peoples within these nations who refused to leave.

### EVIDENCE RECORD CARD

Map of the Indian and Oklahoma territories

**LEVEL** Primary source
**MATERIAL** Map on paper
**LOCATION** Indian and Oklahoma territories of the United States in 1892
**DATE** May 1892
**SOURCE** Library of Congress Geography and Map Division

▲ A Map of the Indian and Oklahoma Territories, published in 1892, shows territories or "reservations" where different Native nations were relocated to.

*"I was sent as interpreter ... in May, 1838, and witnessed the execution of the most brutal order in the History of American Warfare. I saw helpless Cherokees arrested and dragged from their homes, and driven at the bayonet point into the stockades."*

American soldier and interpreter, John G. Burnett, 1890

## THE FIGHT AGAINST DISPLACEMENT

Some Native nations refused to sign treaties that gave all of their land to the U.S. government, choosing instead to fight against displacement. Some battled in courts of law. Others gave up parts of their land, hoping that the government would allow them to live on a smaller portion of it. Some confederations of Native nations waged full-out wars against U.S. forces. In the end, no matter how brave or how just the fight, Native peoples were forced from their lands.

## CHEROKEE NATION BATTLES IN COURT

The Aniyunwiya (Cherokee) fought their battle against displacement in the U.S. Supreme Court in the 1830s. In 1827 Cherokees claimed to be their own **sovereign**, or self-governed, nation and wrote a **constitution** that made it illegal to sell Cherokee lands. Cherokee peoples were one of a group of nations referred to by Europeans as the "five civilized tribes," so-called because they had changed to live lifestyles similar to the "civilized" Europeans. Successful Cherokee farmers were often bullied by Europeans who stole their animals, burned their homes, or **squatted** or moved onto their land.

In 1828 the state of Georgia—where many Cherokee lived—passed laws that

### ANALYZE THIS

This print of John Ross was published about five years after the Cherokees' forced removal. Does Ross appear to be assimilated? What makes you think so? What are the advantages and disadvantages of assimilation?

JOHN ROSS.
A CHEROKEE CHIEF.

*"Our (Cherokee nations) property may be plundered before our eyes; violence may be committed on our persons; even our lives may be taken away, and there is none to regard our complaints. . . . We have neither land nor home, nor resting place that can be called our own."*

Cherokee leader, John Ross, September 18, 1836

▲ This lithograph print of John Ross was produced in 1843. He is holding a paper entitled "Protest and Memorial of the Cherokee Nation Sept. 1836."

took away the rights of the Cherokee peoples and gave power to the state to have them removed from their lands.

Cherokee leader John Ross took the legal battle "Cherokee Nation v. Georgia" to the U.S. Supreme Court in 1831. Cherokees argued that they were a sovereign nation who did not have to live by Georgia state laws.

The court ruled against the Cherokee, saying that they were dependent on the United States.

In 1832, a small group of Cherokee peoples formed a "treaty party" to sell Cherokee lands to the U.S. government. On December 29, 1835, the Cherokee treaty party signed the Treaty of New Echota. This removal treaty with the government stated that the Cherokee must leave their lands by May 12, 1838. Ross, and about 15,000 Cherokee peoples, desperately tried to undo this treaty, but the U.S. government refused. Soldiers forcefully removed Cherokee peoples who refused to leave their homes.

◀ The first edition of the *Cherokee Phoenix* was printed in English and Cherokee script on February 21, 1828

## WARS AGAINST DISPLACEMENT

Native peoples were displaced from areas all across North America including Canada and the southern, central, and western states of the United States. Native nations, such as the Seminoles, the Nimipu (Nez Perce), Ndee (Apache), Nehiyawok (Cree), Lakota (Lakota Sioux), Dine'e (Navajo), Tsitsistas (Cheyenne), Hinonoeino (Arapaho), Numinu (Comanche), Gaigwu (Kiowa), and others, refused to give up their homelands. They fought battles and wars against the Europeans and the U.S. Army. In the end, after thousands of deaths on both sides, and sometimes years of conflict, the United States government won.

### ANALYZE THIS

Irish-American artist Charles Russel was well known for his paintings of the American Civil War and Custer's Last Rally. By studying *Custer's Last Rally* below, who do you think the artist saw his main audience as being? Do you see any Europeans in detail in this painting? Why do you think that is? Do you think Russel sympathized with the Europeans or with the Native peoples?

*"This war was brought upon us by the children of the Great Father who came to take our land from us without a price."*

Lakota Sioux leader Spotted Tail, 1876

▲ *Custer's Last Rally*, showing Native Americans on horseback at the Battle of Little Bighorn, painted by Charles M. Russel in around 1903.

## BLACK HILLS WAR

Europeans also settled out west, especially after gold was discovered. In the 1860s thousands of Native peoples and Europeans were killed in battles and massacres in Minnesota and in the Dakota, Montana, and Wyoming territories. In 1868 the Treaty of Fort Laramie promised western South Dakota, which included the Black Hills region, as a reservation for Sioux peoples. In 1874, after gold was discovered in the area, thousands of Europeans ignored the treaty and moved to the Black Hills. Instead of honoring the treaty, the U.S. government tried to get the Lakota Sioux to sell the Black Hills. In 1876 a confederation of Lakota Sioux, Tsitsistas (Cheyenne), and others fought the U.S. Army in the Black Hills War (1876–1877). On June 25, 1876, the Native Confederacy defeated the U.S. Army in the Battle of Little Big Horn (also called Custer's Last Stand), but were later forced to surrender. The government created a treaty to remove the Lakota Sioux from the Black Hills. Only a few Lakota signed it.

### PERSPECTIVES

Eagle Bonnet was an artist who recorded historic events for his Ogala Sioux Tribe. How is Eagle Bonnet's painting similar or different from Russel's? Can you see where Eagle Bonnet might be biased?

▼ **Chief Crazy Horse (center with spotted war paint) at the Battle of Little Bighorn on June 25, 1876, as painted by Eagle Bonnet, an Oglala Sioux artist from the Pine Ridge Reservation.**

## DISPLACEMENT IN CANADA

In 1867, the British North America Act transferred the job of governing Canada from the British to the Canadians. In 1870, the Canadian government purchased Rupert's Land—a large area of Canada owned by the Hudson's Bay Company (HBC)—and created more Canadian provinces. Native peoples and nations, such as the Métis, Nehiyawok (Cree) and Nakoda (Assiniboine) and many others lived on these lands.

## THE RED RIVER REBELLION

A colony of Métis peoples, led by Louis Riel, lived at the Red River Colony in what is today the Canadian province of Manitoba. The Métis were governed by the HBC. In 1869, the Canadian government surveyed the Metis' land for the upcoming purchase. The Métis were afraid of losing their farmlands to the Canadian government.

They formed a **provisional** government and drew up a bill of rights for the Métis. One of the rights was to join Canada as a province and enjoy the same rights as other provinces.

Riel's men also captured Canadians who were staying nearby and imprisoned them at a nearby fort. One Canadian, Thomas Scott, was put on trial, found guilty, and executed. The Canadian government was furious and offered $5,000 for Riel's capture.

*"Oh my Métis people! You complain that your lands have been stolen. Why, how can it be that you have not yet recovered them?"*

Louis Riel, *The Diaries of Louis Riel,* March 1885

▲ This engraving was published on the front cover of the *Canadian Illustrated News* on April 23, 1870. It shows the execution of Canadian, Thomas Scott, by a Métis soldier.

Canada's French peoples sided with Riel. The English wanted revenge for Scott's death. On May 12, 1870, the area became the province of Manitoba. The Métis were given the rights they wanted. Riel and his people had won their first **rebellion**.

## THE NORTH-WEST REBELLION

Riel fled shortly after to the United States to escape Canadian soldiers but returned to Saskatchewan in 1884 to help Métis peoples rebel against the Canadian government once again. On March 18, 1885 Riel and his men formed a provisional government and demanded that the North-West Mounted Police (NWMP) surrender their fort to Riel and his followers. The NWMP had much more ammunition and forces than Riel. They refused. After two months of fighting, the Métis surrendered in May 1885. Riel was charged with treason and executed.

### ANALYZE THIS

Sydney Prior Hall was a British reportage artist, which is someone who draws reports on an event for journals such as newspapers and magazines. Do you think Hall was present at the time of the actual event? What bias would Hall bring to this painting?

▼ Sydney Prior Hall's painting is titled *The Last Indian Council Held on Canadian Soil Between the Governor-General and Crowfoot, Chief of the Blackfoot Indians, 1881.*

## SCHOOLS FOR NATIVE PEOPLES

Canada's Indian Act of 1876 stated that all lands belonged to the Canadian government, which would distribute it to Native peoples through Ministry of Indian Affairs' agents. The act was designed to assimilate Native peoples. Further amendments to the act did not allow Native peoples to practice their culture and traditions such as spiritual dances or gatherings. Native children were forcefully removed from their families and sent to live and be educated at residential schools. Frightened and homesick children were punished for speaking their native languages and were forced to speak only English. All children had their hair cut short and were made to wear uniforms. Many suffered physical, mental, and sexual abuse while at residential schools. Some children even died. The last residential school in Canada closed in 1996.

## "KILL THE INDIAN AND SAVE THE MAN"

The U.S. Bureau of Indian Affairs began to establish boarding schools for the purpose of assimilating the children of Native peoples. The first boarding school—the Carlisle Indian School—was located in Carlisle, Pennsylvania. It was founded in 1879 by Colonel Richard Henry Pratt, who coined the term, "Kill the Indian, save the man." By this he meant to remove Native peoples' cultural identity from them through the boarding school system.

### ANALYZE THIS

Does anyone in this new group of students look like they want to get their photograph taken? How do you think they feel about having just arrived at the Carlisle Indian Industrial School? Do you think they all feel the same way?

*". . . according to the constitution of the tribes and the distribution of clans, Potlatch, . . . is a necessity, from an Indian point of view, in order to preserve the unity, distinctions and traditions of the race. . ."*

J.B. McCullagh, *The Indian Potlatch*, 1889

▲ This group of Apache students were sent to the Carlisle Indian Industrial School in Carlisle, Pennsylvania, in the late 1800s or early 1900s.

Native children at boarding schools all across the country were removed from their homes, parents, and traditions.

The school system destroyed native children's identities. Children were given new names, forced to speak only English, and made to give up their cultural customs. They were taught American history with a European bias. Many reported being physically, mentally, and sexually abused while attending these schools. Native children were forced to attend boarding schools until the Indian Child Welfare Act was passed in 1978.

## THE DAWES ACT OF 1887

The U.S. government worked toward assimilating Native peoples. After 1870, it created reservations that kept Native peoples in certain areas and allowed Europeans to settle most of the land. Native peoples living on reservations were expected to farm and to convert to Christianity. The government passed laws that banned Native customs. In 1887, the U.S. government passed the Dawes Severalty Act that took away large community reservations and gave smaller parcels of land to individual Native peoples. Most of the lands were sold to Europeans. In the following years, half of Native peoples sold or lost land.

► A classroom at the Carlisle Indian Industrial School, Carlisle, Pennsylvania.

**EVIDENCE RECORD CARD**

Classroom at the Carlisle Indian Industrial School
**LEVEL** Primary source
**MATERIAL** Hand-colored photograph by Frances Benjamin Johnston
**LOCATION** Pennsylvania
**DATE** 1902
**SOURCE** Topfoto

# DIFFERENT VIEWS

*"For nearly 300 years, white Americans, in our zeal to carve out a nation made to order, have dealt with the Indians on the (incorrect), yet tragic, assumption that the Indians were a dying race—to be (killed off). We took away their best lands; broke treaties, promises; tossed them the most nearly worthless scraps of a continent that had once been wholly theirs."*

John Collier,"Report of the Secretary of the Interior for the Fiscal Year Ended June 30, 1938"

Some Native peoples supported assimilation. Brulé Sioux leader Spotted Tail had fought U.S. Army soldiers in many battles. He surrendered in 1855 and was taken prisoner. While imprisoned he was taught how to read and write English. He realized that the Native peoples could not win against the Europeans. He became pro-assimilationist, which means he supported assimilation. He was released from prison in 1856 and returned as a leader of his tribe. In 1877, after the Black Hills War, Spotted Tail helped negotiate the Black Hills Treaty and convinced Lakota Sioux leader Crazy Horse to surrender. American soldiers killed Crazy Horse shortly after. Many blamed Spotted Tail for his death. In 1881, a relative of Crazy Horse named Crow Dog shot and killed Spotted Tail.

Not all Europeans believed that Native peoples were uncivilized. Some fought for Native peoples' rights and believed that their culture should not be destroyed. John Collier was commissioner of the U.S. Bureau of Indian Affairs from 1933 to 1945, and he opposed forced assimilation for Native peoples. Collier went on to promote the Indian Reorganization Act of 1934. Also called the Indian New Deal, this act helped reverse some of the United States' assimilation policies.

▼ The Treaty of Fort Laramie was drawn up at a convention in Wyoming in 1868. The men in this photograph were part of the convention. Notice that the Native participants are each holding a pipe. Do any of the European participants carry a pipe as well?

This cover for a French newspaper shows Nez Perce leader Chief Joseph dying in September 1904. Chief Joseph gained popularity as a brave warrior who resisted displacement and led his people in the Nez Perce War in 1877. What does the fact of his death making the cover of a newspaper in France say about his popularity? What is the mood of the people in the illustration? Are they all Native peoples?

LES DERNIERS PEAUX-ROUGES
Mort de Joseph, le grand chef des « Nez-Percés »

▶ *Le Petit Journal* ("The Small Newspaper") ran this cover on October 9, 1904.

## LAND DISPUTES TODAY

The Oka Crisis was a local land dispute in Canada that grew into a **standoff** between a Mohawk group and government soldiers. It happened in the town of Oka, Quebec, an area the Mohawks believed rightfully belonged to them. In 1961, a golf course was planned for land the Mohawk claimed was their burial grounds. The Mohawk claim was ignored and the golf course was built. In 1990, land developers planned to make the golf course larger and to construct 60 condominiums. Despite further protests, the project was again allowed to go ahead.

In response, a Mohawk protest group **barricaded** the road leading to the golf course. Police officers arrived on July 11, 1990, and used tear gas against the protestors. A fight broke out between officers and the protestors resulting in one officer being shot and killed. Who fired the fatal shot was never officially determined.

▼ Tension between Native peoples and Canadian soldiers ran high at Oka, Quebec, when Mohawk and other Native peoples protested a golf course being expanded near a sacred Native burial site.

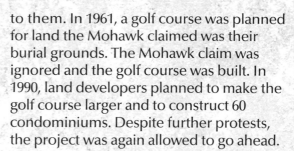

### ANALYZE THIS

A Mohawk warrior stares at a Canadian soldier on September 2, 1990. Can you tell which figure in this photograph is the Mohawk warrior and which is the soldier? What is the soldier carrying? Look at the people in the background of the two figures in green. Many appear to be holding cameras and microphones. Who are these people and what do you think they are doing there?

> "The Sioux tribes have always maintained that confiscation was illegal and the tribes must have some of their ancestral lands returned to them, and they've maintained that position since 1877."
>
> Mario Gonzalez, General Council for the Oglala Sioux tribe, August 24, 2011

Canadian soldiers were brought in to end the standoff and other Native peoples joined the Mohawk protest. The barricade remained for three months until protestors surrendered on September 26, 1990.

## BLACK HILLS LAND DISPUTE

Sioux peoples are still fighting for the Black Hills land. The dispute goes back to the 1868 Treaty of Fort Laramie that gave the Sioux peoples the Black Hills. However, after gold was discovered there, the U.S. government drew up another treaty. Some Sioux signed the new treaty, but there was never enough support to make it legal.

▼ Lakota Sioux are still fighting to reclaim the Black Hills land treatied to them in the Treaty of Fort Laramie in 1868.

The government pushed the treaty through anyway and claimed the land. As a result, the Sioux took the U.S. government to court. In 1980, the Supreme Court ruled in favor of the Sioux and awarded them $102 million. The Sioux, however, have never collected the award. They want the land, not the money.

### ANALYZE THIS

Look at the mountains in the background of this photograph. The sculptures on Mount Rushmore represent the birth, growth, development, and preservation of the United States. Do you think Native peoples feel the same way about what the sculptures represent? Why or why not?

# DISPLACEMENT TODAY

*"It was during this campaign that thousands of women, children, and men were buried in mass graves in many locations. . . . The natives of Kurdistan suffered very hard living conditions, forced relocation and illegal detention for a large number of people."*

Iraqi High Tribunal judge Raid Juhi, *New York Times*, April 5, 2006

Displacement of Native peoples still takes place today all over the world. Kurdish people have lived in the Middle East region since ancient times. Millions live in the southeastern area of Turkey known as Kurdistan. Kurdistan also includes parts of Iraq, Syria, and Iran. Turkey made it illegal for the Kurds to speak or educate their children in their native language. Beginning in 1984, a Kurdish military group wanted to make Kurdistan an independent state. The Turkish military fought against them. It destroyed thousands of Kurdish villages and displaced millions of people from their homes.

From the late 1970s in Iraq, hundreds of thousands of Kurdish people were displaced from the oil fields in Kurdistan around Kirkuk. During the Iran–Iraq war of 1980–1988, Iraq destroyed thousands of Kurdish villages and murdered more than 200,000 Kurdish people. A Kurdish uprising in 1991 led to hundred of thousands of Kurdish families leaving their homes.

In Syria it is illegal to speak the Kurdish language. Kurdish children are not allowed to attend Syrian schools, and Kurdish schools are simply not allowed. Books and documents written in the Kurdish language are banned. Kurdish people are not allowed citizenship and have no rights. Places with Kurdish names were renamed with Arabic names. During the Syrian Civil War (2011 to the present), millions of Kurdish people have been displaced from their homes.

▶ A Syrian Kurdish woman crosses the border with her children in September 2014.

**ANALYZE THIS**

Look at the expressions on the faces of this woman and her children. What do you think the woman is feeling? What are the children feeling? What is the little girl carrying? Look at the men in the background of the photograph. Are they carrying weapons? Is this a dangerous situation? Why or why not?

## STEPS TOWARD HEALING THE PAST

In North America, groups of Native peoples have created organizations to protest land disputes, environmental misuse of Native peoples' lands, and treaties that have been changed or broken. They fight for their rights, which includes equal government funding for education and housing. Many of these organizations work toward righting these wrongs by getting Native peoples and others to join the fight.

## IDLE NO MORE

One of these groups is called Idle No More. The Canadian-based organization is protesting the Canadian government's efforts to pass laws so that companies can purchase reserve lands to profit from their natural resources. Idle No More members hold **teach-ins**, rallies, and protests to make Canadians aware of these issues.

### PERSPECTIVES

A 2015 report into missing and murdered aboriginal women found that the Canadian police forces have "failed to adequately prevent and protect indigenous women and girls from killings and disappearances." Even though the tragedies have been occurring for more than 20 years, the Canadian government is only now just beginning to take steps toward stopping violence against aboriginal women.

▼ Protestors perform a drumming ceremony in 1999 after a memorial for 23 Aboriginal women who have gone missing in British Columbia.

## GOVERNMENT APOLOGIES

Both Canada and the United States have started to take small steps to address the many wrongs that their respective governments have done to their Native peoples from the time of early colonization up to today. On June 11, 2008, the Canadian prime minister Stephen Harper gave a public apology to Canadian Native peoples for Canada's residential school and forced assimilation policy. In the United States, President Barack Obama signed the Native American Apology Resolution Bill into law in 2009.

Even though government leaders have admitted breaking promises and treating Native peoples wrongly throughout their history, many Native peoples feel the apologies are too little and have come too late. Many do not trust that new promises made to correct the wrongs of the past will be fulfilled. Considering the primary source records of the past, do you believe they are wrong in not trusting the government?

▲ John Parsons, aka Tyhogeñhs, holds a wampum belt commissioned by President Washington after signing a treaty with the Onondaga in 1794. The Onondaga claim that since then, 2.5 million acres of land have been stolen from them by New York State.

*"Our People and our Mother Earth can no longer afford to be economic hostages in the race to industrialize our homelands. It's time for our People to rise up and take back our role as caretakers and stewards of the land."*

Eriel Deranger, Athabasca Chipewyan First Nations

# TIMELINE

**1492** Christopher Columbus discovers the Americas

**1794** Battle of Fallen Timbers; conflict between Native Confederacy and U.S. Army

**1795** Treaty of Greenville gives Ohio and parts of Indiana to the United States

**1812—1814** War between British Loyalists and U.S. Patriots

**1831** Cherokee leader John Ross battles the State of Georgia over land rights in the U.S. Supreme Court: the court ruled against the Cherokees

**1867** The British North America Act transfers control of Canada from the British to the Canadians

**1870** Canadian government makes the Red River area a full province of Canada, with land grants to the Métis

**1876** The Indian Act of 1876 is passed into law in Canada, assimilating the Native peoples

**1879** First Boarding School for Native peoples is opened

**1885** Riel leads North-West Rebellion but is defeated, tried, and executed

**1492**

**1800**

**1835**

**1875**

**1899**

**1500s** European settlers begin to arrive in the Americas

**1775—1783** American Revolution: United States wins independence from Great Britain

**1809** Treaty of Fort Wayne gives 3 million acres of land in Indiana to U.S. government

**1830** Indian Removal Act of 1830 is signed by U.S. president Andrew Jackson, forcing the removal of Native peoples across the U.S.; Native People journey to the Indian Territory along the Trail of Tears

**1835** A small group of Cherokee form a Treaty Party and sign the Treaty of New Echota to leave their lands

**1868** Red River Rebellion led by Louis Riel

**1868** Treaty of Fort Laramie is signed between U.S. government and the Sioux, giving the Sioux South Dakota and the Black Hills

**1874** Gold is discovered in the Black Hills

**1876** Black Hills War is fought between Native peoples and U.S. Army

**1884** Riel returns to Canada from exile in the U.S.

**1887** The Dawes Severalty Act is passed, giving the U.S. government power to abolish large community reservations and give smaller parcels of land to individuals

**1900**

**1934** Indian Reorganization Act of 1934 helps to reverse some U.S. assimilation policies

**1980** U.S. Supreme Court awards the Sioux $1.3 billion dollars for the Black Hills, which the Sioux refuse; negotiations continue in 2016

**1990** Oka Crisis; Mohawks protest the expansion of a golf course on sacred lands

**2008** Canadian prime minister Stephen Harper publically apologizes to Native peoples for residential schools and assimilation policies

**2010** U.S. president Barack Obama signs the North American Apology Resolution Bill into law

**2015**

▼ **The displacement of Native peoples in the United States during the 1800s.**

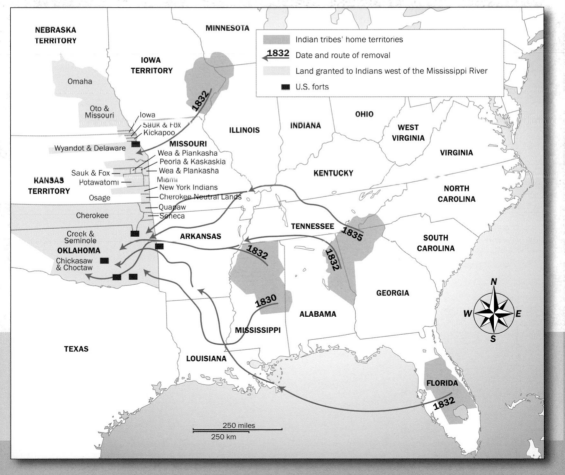

# BIBLIOGRAPHY

## QUOTATIONS AND INTERVIEWS

p. 4  Canassatego, circa 1740.
www.smithsoniansource.org/display/primarysource
/viewdetails.aspx?PrimarySourceID=1195

p. 6  Massasoit, circa 1600.
http://archive.adl.org/education/curriculum_conne
ctions/na_quotes.html

p. 8
Parkman, Francis. *The Oregon Trail*, 1846.

p. 10
Hopkins, John Castell. *The Story of the Dominion*,
1901.

p. 12
Santana. U.S. Bureau of Ethnography Annual
Report, 17th, 1895-1896.
www.smithsoniansource.org/display/primarysource
/viewdetails.aspx?PrimarySourceId=1018

p. 14
Sun Elk. Native American Testimony. 1999.
The Commonwealth (Wisconsin) Frankfort, July 2,
1833. Actual primary source document found at
www.wisconsinhistory.org/Content.aspx?dsNav=N:4
294963828-
4294963788&dsRecordDetails=R:BA13613

p. 16
Parkman, Francis. *The Oregon Trail*, 1846.

p. 18
Bouquet, Henry. Excerpt from a letter dated July 13,
1763. Find the actual document at:
www.nativeweb.org/pages/legal/amherst/34_40_
305_fn.jpeg

p. 20
Onundaga'ono (Oneida) member. American
Archives, 4th series, volume 2, 1839.
http://edsitement.neh.gov/sites/edsitement.neh.go
v/files/worksheets/Oneida%20annotated.pdf

p. 22
Tecumseh, Speech at Tuckaubatchee, 1811.
www.indigenouspeople.net/tecumseh.htm

p. 24
Burnett, John G. Letter written in 1890.
www.learnnc.org/lp/editions/nchist-
newnation/4532
Wahnenauhi. Personal account.
www.digitalhistory.uh.edu/disp_textbook.cfm?smtID
=3&psid=1147

p. 26
Ross, John. Excerpt from letter written in 1836.
www./pbs.org/wgbh/aia/part4/4h3083t.html

p. 28
Spotted Tail.
www.archives.gov/exhibits/american_originals/indu
stry.html

p. 30 Reil, Louis. *The Diaries of Louis Riel*. March
1885.

p. 32
McCullagh, J. B. *The Indian Potlatch*, 1899. Found
at :
http://eco.canadiana.ca/view/oocihm.15538/2?r=
0&s=1

p. 34
Collier, John. "Report of the Secretary of the Interior
for the Fiscal Year Ended June 30, 1938." Found at:
https://archive.org/details/annualreportofse8231u
nit

p. 36
Juhi, Raid. *The New York Times*, April 5, 2006.
Found at: -
www.nytimes.com/2006/04/05/world/05iht-sadda
m.html?pagewanted=all&_r=0

p. 38
Gonzalez, Mario. PBS News Hour. August 24, 2011.
Found at:
http:/pbs.org/newshour/updates/north_america-
july-dec11-blackhills_08-23/

p. 40
Deranger, Eriel. Found at:
www.idlenomore.ca
Harper, Stephen. Statement of apology to former
students of Indian Residential Schools. June 11,
2008. Found at: www.aadnc-aandc.gc.ca/eng/
1100100015644/1100100015649
Obama, Barack. Remarks by the president at the
White House Tribal Nations Conference. December
16, 2010. Found at: www.whitehouse.gov/the-press-
office/2010/12/16/remarks-president-white-house
-tribal-nations-conference

# INTERNET GUIDELINES

Finding good source material on the Internet can sometimes be a challenge. When analyzing how reliable the information is, consider these points:

- Who is the author of the page? Is it an expert in the field or a person who experienced the event?
- Is the site well-known and up to date? A page that has not been updated for several years probably has out-of-date information.
- Can you verify the facts with another site? Always double check information.

- Have you checked all possible sites? Don't just look on the first page a search engine provides. Remember to try government sites and research papers.
- Have you recorded website addresses and names? Keep this data so you can backtrack and verify the information you want to use.

## TO FIND OUT MORE

**Non-Fiction:**
Ellis, Deborah: *Looks Like Daylight: Voices of Indigenous Kids*. Groundwood Books, 2013.

January, Brendan. *Native Americans*. Raintree, 2005.

Neil, Philip: *The Great Circle: A History of the First Nations*. Clarion Books, 2006.

Paleja, Shaker Natvar. *Native Americans: A Visual Exploration*. Annick Press, 2013.

Paul, Daniel. *We Are Not Savages: Collision between European and Native American Civilizations*. National Geographic Society, 2004.

**Historical Fiction:**
Bruchac, Joseph. *Eagle Song*. Puffin Books, 1999.

Bruchac, Joseph. *Navajo Long Walk: The Tragic Story of a People's Forced March from their Homeland*. National Geographic Society, 2002.

Erdrich, Louise. *The Birchbark House*. Disney-Hyperion, 2002.

## WEBSITES

**Native American history and primary sources:**
www.loc.gov

**Great resource for primary sources and historical background:**
www.archives.gov/research/alic/reference/native-americans.html

**The Red Rebellion and North-West Rebellion:**
www.metisnation.org/culture--heritage/louis-riel

**Idle No More:**
www.idlenomore.ca/

**Canadian Residential School History:**
http://indigenousfoundations.arts.ubc.ca/home/government-policy/the-residential-school-system.html

**Native peoples' history in Canada:**
www.aadnc-aandc.gc.ca

# GLOSSARY

**Aboriginal** People who have lived in an area from earliest times

**American Indian** Natives peoples named because their land was originally thought by Christopher Columbus to be India

**ancestry** Relatives who have lived in the past

**artifacts** Objects of historical interest made by humans

**assimilate** To make a person or group of people live within a culture that is not their own

**authority** The right to make decisions for a group of people

**barricade** To block and not allow people or supplies to enter or leave

**bias** Prejudice in favor of or against one thing, person, or group compared with another

**captive** Held against a person's will

**Christianity** A religious belief that Jesus Christ is the son of God

**chronology** A record of events that have happened at different times during a long period

**civilize** To live in an organized manner with shared systems of beliefs and traditions

**colonist** A person who settles in and lives in a colony

**colony** An area partially controlled or governed by a distant country and usually settled by people from that country

**confederacy** A group of people who join together to achieve a common goal

**confiscate** To take away one's property

**constitution** Written laws and principles by which a country is governed

**context** The circumstances or setting in which an event happens

**convention** A large meeting or conference where a formal treaty or agreement is reached

**convert** To change a person's beliefs

**culture** The arts and other achievements of a certain society

**descendant** A relative of others who lived in the past

**detention** To be held in prison

**displaced** Removed

**displacement** The often enforced removal of people from their homes and lands

**document** Something written or printed on paper

**emigrate** To leave a country permanently to live elsewhere

**enslave** To force a person to become a slave

**era** A long period of history with a distinct characteristic

**evaluate** To form an idea about

**evidence** The body of facts or information to show whether something is true

**excerpt** A small part of a larger written, spoken, or filmed record

**export** To sell a product from one country to another

**First Nations** Native peoples of Canada who are not Métis or Inuit

**First Peoples** Aboriginal peoples living in North America

**historian** A person who studies history

**history** The record of a particular time or event that has happened in the past

**homeland** The place where a person was born or has lived for most of their lives

**immigrant** A person who enters a country to live there permanently

**immunity** The ability to remain healthy and not be infected with diseases

**independent** To be free of someone else's rule

**indigenous** Originating from, and belonging to, an area or place

**interpret** To explain the meaning of something

# GLOSSARY

**interpreter** A person who translates one language for a person who does not understand that language

**Inuit** Indigenous peoples of Northern Canada

**investigate** To ask questions and study something to find out the truth

**Métis** A person of mixed indigenous and European ancestry

**missionaries** People sent on a religious mission

**native** Born in a particular area or place

**Native American** A term that originated in the 1960s to replace American Indian

**negotiate** To discuss a situation from both sides to form an agreement

**neutral** A person or country that does not take sides in a conflict

**offensive** Rude and inappropriate

**pilgrim** A person who travels abroad for religious reasons; the Pilgrim Fathers sailed to America in 1620 to escape religious persecution in England

**potlatch** A traditional ceremony for First Nations who usually live on Canada's west coast

**preserved** Kept in its original condition

**primary source** A firsthand account or direct evidence of an event

**provisional** Formed for a short time only and likely to change

**rebellion** An organized effort to change an existing government by protesting or using violent means

**Redskin** An offensive term for Native peoples that has been used for hundreds of years

**refugee** Someone forced to leave their home because of things beyond their control such as war or natural or manmade disasters

**reliable** A person or thing that can be trusted

**relocate** To move from one area to another

**reservation** An area of land set aside by a country's government for Native peoples to live on

**resolution** An official answer to a problem

**resources** Land, minerals, and other raw materials of use to people

**revoke** To stop or cancel an existing law

**savage** Wild and untamed; as a noun, also an offensive term for a Native person

**secondary source** Material created by studying primary sources

**slave** A person owned by another and treated as property, without any rights

**sovereign** A country that governs itself

**squat** To live on another person's land without the authority to do so

**squaw** An offensive name for a young, Native female

**standoff** A deadlock between two opponents

**stockade** A holding area with walls formed by stakes

**symbolize** A symbol or thing that stands for a larger idea

**teach-in** A session held to educate people about an issue

**technology** Equipment developed through scientific knowledge

**tomahawk** An ax used by Native Americans as a weapon

**treaty** An official government document that gives the rules by which two or more parties will live by

**wampum beads** Small shells used as currency, jewelry, and to decorate or write messages on materials

**wretched** Poor and miserable conditions

# INDEX